REMARRIED *with* CHILDREN...

Questions And Answers for Happier Stepfamilies

By
Stephen H. Wilson, M.A.
M. Karen Kegelmeyer, M.S.
Alan Dupre-Clark, D. Min.

Introducing: **THE FIVE-FACTOR SELF-ESTEEM METHOD FOR STEPPARENTING**

DEDICATION

For our original families and the families we have become.

For Peggy, Tony, and Lori.

For Pam, whose steadfast support seems to make everything possible.

ACKNOWLEDGMENTS

We gratefully acknowledge the contributions and help of all of the stepfamilies with whom we have worked. It is from them that we have been able to discern many of the concepts presented in this book.

We are especially grateful to Sheila and Dennis Mellman for their encouragement, support, and persistence. They were there at the beginning of our development of stepfamily resources. The Mellmans are great examples of how, out of pain and chaos can come harmony and joy for a stepfamily.

Our heartfelt appreciation to Susan Willson-Brooks and the staff of The Elizabeth Blackwell Center, Columbus, Ohio, for their confidence in our vision and for making a place for stepfamilies.

Thanks to Michael Senett for lending his creative genius to the design of this book.

"Remarried With Children: Questions And Answers For Happier Stepfamilies"
is a publication of

Ohio Professional Counseling Services, Inc.
3400 N. High Street
Suite 120
Columbus, Ohio 43202
(800) 669-5233

First Printing 1992
ISBN: 0-9632900-0-2

CONTENTS

You may give them your love but not your thoughts.
For they have their own thoughts.
You may house their bodies but not their souls,
for their souls dwell in the house of tomorrow,
which you cannot visit, not even in your dreams.

--Kahlil Gibran

Now there's a new group called Marriage Anonymous.
If you feel like proposing, you call up this number
and an orthodontist quotes you his rates.

--Robert Orben

INTRODUCTION

"It's easy to be a stepparent. All you need is the wisdom of Solomon, the patience of Job, and the financial resources of an Arabian oil sheik!"
                                    --Anonymous Stepparent

This book has evolved from a combined total of more than fifty years of professional experience with stepfamilies in a clinical therapy setting, and several years of conducting discussion groups, classes, and seminars on the subject. The questions have been assimilated from those actually heard and from reading between the lines of the dilemmas that are repeatedly presented to us. The answers to the questions have been drawn from our counseling experience with stepfamilies, from other practitioners in the field, and from our personal experiences. The authors' perspectives and experiences about stepfamilies arise from a broad spectrum of family lifestyles. We are compelled by our personal and professional experiences to offer this book.

Our Personal Stepfamily Experiences

Steve acquired a stepmother at age 25 and became a stepfather at age 43, when he married Pam. Their blended family includes Pam's two children and two of Steve's three children--all living in the same household. Alan married Peggy when he was age thirty, and became a stepfather of two children. He has no children from a previous marriage. Karen became an adult stepdaughter at age thirty-one when her father remarried; they are blending five children and fourteen grandchildren as a stepfamily.

We came to our stepfamilies as a result of surviving a variety of traumas including disease and death, father abandonment, and suicide. Although the paths to stepfamily life have been very different for each of us, we have certain things in common with each other, and perhaps with you.

Among the similarities: Like many stepfamilies, in the process of blending, members were added to our lives bringing separate histories with them which we do not share. And, not every family member welcomed the opportunity to become a part of the new family. We each experienced some grief about the loss of a previous family or the loss of the fantasy of the family we had hoped to have. We face the reality of the newly blended family with a mixture of apprehension and hope. Also, we are struggling to do our best in roles that are not easily or clearly defined, relying on instinct and feelings to guide us. Through the good fortune of a close working relationship, we have also supported one another. We are forging some directions that make sense to us.

We have seen people go into marriages believing that, having been married, they *should* be able to make another marriage work just fine. The problem is that the wisdom gained from the first experience does not necessarily exactly apply. This is especially true if the subsequent marriage involves children in any way; the issues and dynamics in a stepfamily are different from those in a biological/nuclear family. We know that there are many questions and challenges facing the blending family. This book presents practical, open and honest answers to a collection of those questions that face virtually everyone involved in stepfamily life. You are not alone. This book responds to the legitimacy of stepfamily dilemmas, and promotes further inquiry into solutions.

Considering that 70 million Americans are involved in stepfamily relationships and 9,000 stepfamilies form each week, stepfamilies need and deserve extra assistance to properly prepare and support them for the challenges ahead.

The Structure of This Book

In the section following this introduction we present our ideas about a new view of stepparenting which we believe will bring relief to those wrestling with these challenges. It is time for the special needs of stepfamilies to receive the attention they deserve. Stepfamilies are very different from "biological" families in a number of significant ways. Theories of family life and parent-child relationships which may help "natural" families are often useless for stepfamilies.

Having introduced you to a wonderful way of looking at the role of stepparents, we tackle many questions which have been raised by the parents, stepparents, and children in these families. Each question represents an actual question which was asked of us during a workshop, seminar, or therapy session. In some cases the questions are composites of concerns. We have tried to remain faithful to the sense of the concerns as we heard them, and respond in ways that reflect our belief that one of the most practical ways to succeed in stepfamilies is to follow the path of high self-esteem, unconditional positive regard, and value and respect for every person involved.

The language used about stepfamilies is often inconsistent and uncertain. Stepfamilies, blended families, or non-biological nuclear families are all terms referring to the same thing: a two-parent family in which at least one child is not a blood relative of one of the parents. Therefore, we have decided to use a variety of terms: step, blended, natural, real, and birth. In the absence of a single authoritative source on the subject, these words reflect the common terminology of current usage.

Our goal is to bring a multi-purpose, easy-to-use educational tool for adults, children, educators, and clinicians interested in strengthening stepfamily life. We encourage parents to use this resource with each other in study groups or retreats. Reading the children's questions with the children or aloud with the whole family can be a good discussion starter. Talking these over, say, one at a time each night, could be helpful. We encourage children who can, to read the parent's questions. Children will find it helpful to discuss many of these questions with their parents. School or religious groups for children may find it advantageous to use the children's questions as a format. Clinicians can use these questions and answers as a theme for family sessions to stimulate the kind of interaction that is helpful for the family.

Each question and answer is followed by a quotation. The quotations are drawn from a variety of wisdom, folklore, and philosophies regarding families, relationships, and parenting. These have been added as a reminder that previous thinkers on the subject may offer truths that help us find our way through the mazes of living and growing in stepfamilies. They also add a touch of humor which helps us keep our perspec-

touch of humor which helps us keep our perspective.

We hope that these questions and answers will provide you with a rough outline of the territory which is stepfamily life, and that the answers give some measure of direction through the landscape over which many of us are traveling or will travel.

Stephen H. Wilson
M. Karen Kegelmeyer
Alan Dupre-Clark

A NEW VIEW OF STEPPARENTING

Introducing the Five-Factor Self-Esteem Method

The Key To Successful Stepparenting

There are many boondoggles for stepfamilies which have long begged for correction. Some remarried couples have taken advantage of books and classes on the subject to help them get past the frustrations and disappointments (a few of the available resources are listed at the end of this book). There is no common agreement among professionals as to what factors account for or contribute to the successful blending of a stepfamily. This is due, no doubt, to the wide variety of stepfamily structures: remarried after divorce, following a death, your-mine-and our children, acquiring children of all ages including adulthood, multiple remarriages, and more. As a result, the happy stepfamily is the exception rather than the rule, and takes a long time to work out, if it ever does work out.

Extraordinary challenges befall stepfamilies. Blending into new families following the breakup of the previous family puts an incredible strain on everyone concerned, including and perhaps especially the remarriage. These strains have to do with mending broken families and broken dreams, and healing the wound left and often continuing after embittered marital conflicts and legal battles. It is not unusual for there to be layer upon layer of challenges for both adults and children to their healthy emotional growth and stability. These layers include all of the usual tasks of growing into maturity, and finding love, joy, and purpose in life and, in addition, reconciling inequitable financial settlements, forced separations, bereavement, and the cruelest juxtapositions of accusations, lies, denials, and protestations of love.

Stepfamilies are no simple matter. We believe that the task of effectively blending and healing and growing requires a particular set of foundation strengths and an outlook and mindset that can support the emotionally loaded work that is cut out for the family. For example, one of the troublesome challenges and questions that gets us tripped up is, "Can a stepparent be a real parent?"

Our experience helping parents and families leads us to believe that, in order to be effective in a relationship to "someone else's kids," it is neither necessary nor sufficient for stepparents to merely form parent/child relationships in the traditional sense. Even the natural parents should avoid some aspects of traditional parenting, and in their stead, invoke a new and stronger view of self, child and parent.

The recommendations found in this book grow out of our own extensive experiences as well as the work and theories of clinicians and family practitioners such as John Bradshaw, Pia Mellody, Janet Woititz, Claudia Black, Terry Kellogg, and Melody Beattie. We are suggesting that parents and stepparents consider a different-from-the-traditional view of parenting. This new view has its foundation in the current state of knowledge about human physical, emotional, and spiritual development. It is centered on valuing the nature of human existence and all life at the highest level and believing in an ultimately positive human destiny as universal conditions of our species, and our birthright.

We believe that many parenting practices which have traditionally been accepted as "parental rights and responsibilities" are unhealthy. They do not fulfill the proper role of adults toward children. They do not place the highest value on children, are contrary to optimum human development, and do not lead children to become effective and joyful adults.

Compared to other animals, human beings require an extraordinary length of time to achieve maturity (18-25 years). This is a long journey through a developmental minefield which few of us can complete without experiencing a number of explosions and the accompanying injuries. The stepfamily has more than the usual number of bombs waiting to go off. In order for a human infant to arrive at maturity as a joyful and effective adult, there are a number of critical stages which must be passed, many skills to be mastered, and an optimum environment which must be provided. It is the role of adults—whether or not they are the biological parents—to responsibly provide for an environment which respectfully recognizes the needs and values of all human beings and, thereby, honors five conditions which all human beings have in common by virtue of being born into this species. Critical to this view of parenting is that this role is to be fulfilled without shaming the child.

The Five-Factor Self-Esteem Method

We are indebted to Pia Mellody for formulating

this view of human development, and to William J. "Bill" McGrane, C.P.A.E., for his enormous efforts to understand self-esteem and to promote global high self-esteem. For a detailed treatment of the subject, the reader is encouraged to read a description of Mellody's theory and system in her book, *Facing Codependence* (Harper & Row), and any number of books and tapes available from The McGrane Self-Esteem Institute, Cincinnati, Ohio.

In order for any of us to be or become emotionally healthy and fully functioning, there are five factors which require proper, i.e., non-shaming, attention. They are **value, vulnerability, imperfection, dependence,** and **immaturity**. Absence of proper attention to these factors constitutes some degree of abuse (emotional, physical, intellectual, sexual, or spiritual abuses are all possible) which ultimately robs us of the high self-esteem with which we were born. With high self-esteem, happy and successful stepfamilies will be an everyday accomplishment.

What makes this new information difficult to grasp is the fact that many of the characteristics which our society has traditionally valued as desirable are actually unhealthy. Pia Mellody points out, "Our society believes that people who exhibit the characteristics (of codependence) at one extreme--arrogance, invulnerability, perfectionism, antidependence, and 'being in control'--are healthy, well-adjusted adults. However, the pain in their lives from unfulfilling relationships, unsatisfying careers, depression, and other problems would indicate that they are *not* functional adults." They are suffering from various degrees of dis-ease which is estimated to similarly affect 96% of Americans.

In Mellody's description of this dis-ease, which she calls codependence, we can see many of the troubles that beset stepfamilies. As she describes the recovery from codependence, we see many solutions for stepfamilies.

How the Method Works

Any adult can learn about and respond to the five factors which must be nurtured in children. It is not necessary to be the biological parent or have someone call you "mom" or "dad." We believe that, with the five-factor mode of dealing with children, strong relationships that have elements of caring, concern, love, respect, cooperation, and gratitude will be a common occurrence. In this regard, there is a dual task for all of us as parents and stepparents: becoming healthy ourselves in order to be able to foster healthy development in the children for whom we share responsibility.

Commercial air travel provides an apt metaphor for how to approach the five-factor method. If you have been a passenger on an airline you will recall that pre-take-off safety instructions are given by the cabin attendants. When they describe the oxygen mask safety feature they say, "When the oxygen masks are released, if you are with a small child, put your own mask on first, then put the child's mask on." Our instructions for the five-factor method are the same: the parent must understand the factors and apply them personally first, before attempting to apply them to a child. In many cases, the parent may only be one step ahead of the children as all learn together to have high self-esteem, awareness of feelings and safe ways to express them, mutual respect, and to be non-abusive.

We cannot give away that which we have not yet received. It is only when we parents have received the lessons of the five-factors and are working them in our lives, that we can successfully guide the family in such a healthy direction. There is a wise tongue-in-cheek observation that children learn from two things: what their parents do, and what their parents do. In other words, we are all role models and our actions always speak louder than our words. So take this system to heart for yourself as a parent, work with it personally, and you will have the best chance at positive, joyful outcomes with your family.

The Five Factors

Because we are all born *vulnerable*, we need protection and we need to learn how to protect ourselves without offending others. Therefore, parents must model that they can establish effective boundaries so that others cannot abuse them, intimidate them, or control what they think and feel and do. When parents respond to the vulnerability factor in a non-shaming way, the children learn how to protect themselves without harming others, and grow to be adults who can establish and maintain functional boundaries.

Because we are all born *valuable*, (we are products of the highest intelligence in the universe) we are all equally worthy of the highest value. Our value is inherent in our *being*, as opposed to our *doing*. Our society confuses these values and leads us to the erroneous belief that our self-esteem will come from our accomplishments and achievements such as our grades in school, job titles, and material wealth. Striving for this false sense of self-esteem has turned many people into *human doings* who lose touch with their authentic *human being*. Without proper ways to measure our worth, we feel either inferior (less-than) or superior (more-than) rather than equal to others.

Therefore, parents must work to remove any obstacles to their own high self-esteem. Then, when parents respond to the factor of their own and the child's intrinsic value in a non-shaming way, the children can grow to be mature adults with high levels of self-esteem, i.e., an abiding sense of one's own preciousness.

Because we are all born *imperfect*, no matter how well we learn to manage our lives, we never can achieve perfection. We all make mistakes. Functional adults do not strive for perfection, and they have a good-natured, non-value-judging acceptance of their own and other's imperfection.

Therefore, parents must model a non-judgmental, multi-valued view of the world. Then, when parents respond to the factor of their own and the child's imperfection in a non-shaming way, the children can grow to be adults who are comfortable being responsible for imperfections and likely to feel a connection to a Higher Power.

Because we are born *dependent*, we have needs and wants which we cannot meet alone. We require others to help us. The condition of dependence will remain all through our lives. No matter how independent we think we are, we can never satisfy all of our needs and wants without sometimes turning to others for help. Not be able to ask for help, or to feel ashamed for needing help, is dysfunctional (antidependent).

Therefore, parents must work to become comfortable with asking for help and model an interdependent relationship. When parents respond to the factor of their own and the child's dependence in a non-shaming way, the children can grow to be adults who are comfortably interdependent and able to get their needs and wants met appropriately.

Because we are born *immature*, we do not

express our reality moderately. We cry and tantrum, we laugh and giggle hysterically. We grow through the various stages of maturity with the ideal being to act appropriately mature for each age level. Dysfunctional adults continue to have difficulty expressing their reality in moderation, with age-level maturity. They ignore or are out of touch with certain needs, wants, and emotions, or they are overwhelmed by them. Functional adults are able to be moderate about the same things that create chaos, disharmony, and pain for the dysfunctional adult.

Therefore, parents must develop effective (and moderate) ways of expressing their feelings and needs, and the maturity to face reality with a full range of appropriate emotions. Parents must understand that development of maturity is something that occurs in stages over time so as not to demand too much too soon or tolerate too little too long. Then, when parents respond to the maturity factor in a non-shaming way, the children can grow into adults who are mature at their age level.

The Five-Factor Self-Esteem Method respects and values all family members for the most basic qualities and needs inherent in all of us. The Method can be used by any of us, regardless of our biological relationship to each other. Whether or not you are the "natural" parent to a child, following the Five-Factor Self-Esteem Method, you can be an enormous positive influence and foster very satisfying familial relationships in less time than when following the more traditional approach.

THE LEARNING STEPFAMILY: A REVOLUTIONARY APPROACH TO BLENDING

Stepfamilies Are More Than Different

All families must learn how to be a family. Being a family—and especially becoming a stepfamily—is not something that anyone automatically knows how to do. Our learning about how families operate is influenced by a variety of factors and forces. Our own family of origin is one of the strongest influences. Without realizing it, people often assume that their own family's ways, traditions, values, and rituals are the best or right way to be a family. If there is something they didn't like about their family of origin, they erroneously believe they can easily "do it better" when they have a family of their own.

Other factors which shape our ideas about how a family should be conducted include our religious beliefs, ethnicity, the society we are part of, other families we have seen, formal education through family life classes, books, and talking to friends and neighbors (who may be well-meaning but less than completely honest about what's going on behind their closed doors). It has come to light through our work that the media has played a part in giving many people highly unrealistic expectations about family life. We see many who become aware that the frustration and disappointments they experience in their families come from trying to recreate the "Donna Reed" or "Father Knows Best" family.

There cannot be many recipes for stepfamilies because there are so many variations in stepfamily forms and needs. The successful stepfamily of the future will not look for easy, cookie-cutter answers but will seek out, learn, practice, and develop a set of skills which allow it to see itself as unique and enable it to solve the unique challenges it faces. Each family has a different set of circumstances, grief-work, combinations of children, financial structure, emotional homework, dreams and ambitions. Sooner or later, every successful stepfamily must create an effective design for healing the wounds that occurred as part of the circumstances which created the opportunity for a stepfamily in the first place. Creating that effective design requires awareness of and access to *learning tools*.

Stepfamilies must be custom-designed by the parents, and will work best when they are designed for learning—learning how to be a family in which everyone can grow and be supported and loved so that, in spite of whatever may have happened to their previous families, there can be psychological and emotional health within the stepfamily. It might be said that one of the primary purposes of a stepfamily is to learn how to be a stepfamily. And the learning process must include all members of the family, not only the parents.

The kind of learning we are talking about here is not learning in the ordinary sense. It is a kind of learning that is embodied in a word that you don't hear in everyday conversation, but one that is well worth thinking about: "metanoia." It means a shift of mind, and it has to do with learning, but not just any learning or any shift. Metanoia refers to a fundamental shift or change, variously described as "movement of the mind," "transcendence," "awakening shared intuition," and "direct knowing of the highest." In its root meaning it refers to shifting "the mind beyond the mind" ("meta," meaning above or beyond, and "noia," from the root "nous," of mind). In metanoia, you learn something that results in a mind shift which raises your thinking to a higher level, a vantage point from which you have a greater perspective.

Peter Senge, Director of the Systems Thinking and Organizational Learning Program at MIT's Sloan School of Management, observes that "in every day use, learning has come to be synonymous with 'taking in information'" which he says is actually "only distantly related to real learning." "Real learning," according to Senge, "gets to the heart of what it means to be human. Through learning we re-create ourselves. Through learning we become able to do something we never were able to do. Through learning we reperceive the world and our relationship to it. Through learning

we extend our capacity to create, to be part of the generative process of life." And we expand our capacity to create our future. (A more extensive explanation of metanoia and the organizational principles which can be extrapolated to stepfamilies can be found in Senge, Peter M., *The Fifth Discipline: The Art and Practice of the Learning Organization*, Doubleday/Currency, 1990.)

The Tools of The Effective Stepfamily

The successful design of a *learning stepfamily* environment will include or require a set of "tools" which encompass certain knowledge, skills, values, and attitudes. Among them are:

- A belief that one person (parent or child) cannot and does not need to have all of the answers for all of the problems.
- A belief in the value of patiently exploring possibilities and alternatives in every important situation, rather than rushing in with quick-fix solutions.
- A recognition that cooperation will be more effec-

tive than coercion.

- A belief in the stepfamily as a group of people who can learn to care for and about each other, show appreciation, and provide life-long supportive connections.
- A method for seeking input from family members by which democratic approaches are favored over autocratic.
- A willingness to recognize that, no matter how sure you are that you are right, another person, who has a different idea, may be right, too.
- A willingness to seek out and become aware of one's own assumptions and to challenge those assumptions as to the underlying evidence so as to be better prepared for possible outcomes, and to make the best possible decisions when "there are no right answers."
- A commitment to creating a safe environment within the home and family, i.e., one that promotes non-judgmental, non-blaming acceptance along with respect for the individual's right to differ and a strong desire for deeply honest sharing of feelings and opinions. In turn, this will foster a non-defensive openness, a search for "truths," flexibility, and, ultimately, strong support for decisions and direction within a creative problem-solving structure.
- A commitment to overcoming past hurts and getting away from ongoing petty emotional fighting. Most of those who have been through it know that bickering often escalates into all-out "war" complete with the taking up of positions, digging in for the duration, and enlisting the children to conduct espionage. Then there are skirmishes, raids, attacks and counter-attacks the result of which is that, though many battles may be won by either side, the war, if it can be won at all, brings about the destruction of a host of innocent "civilians." And, one of the worst tragedies of all this is the inevitable pressures, especially on the children, to take sides with one parent (or sibling) or the other, inflicting devastating psychological wounds which may never heal.
- A dedication to the best interest of all (individually and collectively) with the highest priorities going to those who are least able to protect themselves and most dependent. Among other things, this means timely, complete, and ungrudging pay-

ment of fair child support, keeping the promise of visitation (in fact, doing one's level best to keep all promises), being a concerned and interested parent even from a distance; and, every adult taking every step necessary to insure their own personal mental health and maturity.

- Unyielding effort on the part of all of the adults whose lives touch the lives of the children to put the past behind and work for a harmonious world, starting with the family. This can only be made possible by skilled and practiced attention to the five factors of self-esteem, which are among the most fundamental conditions of human being, and the conscious practice of forgiveness.

Will It Be Worth The Effort?

The knowledge, skill, values, and attitudinal tools of the learning stepfamily will enable the stepfamily to come to know and understand the unique characteristics with which it must deal, and how to make the best decisions for dealing with them. With this approach the family and its members are much less likely to feel like helpless victims of events and processes which they do not control and will see that they can work together to create a satisfying future, individually and collectively.

Out of this new way--becoming a *learning family*--the children will have the best chances for growing to become effective and joyful adults and then taking powerful tools with them into their own families. And the parents will be able to use the same tools to have the greatest chance at managing the stresses of blending while growing their own intimate and supportive relationship for a lifetime of happiness.

Hope For The Future

The successful stepfamily of the future will be committed to higher values and a greater good. Using the *learning tools* to get beyond pettiness, the effective stepparents of the future will manage their responsibilities with a larger view of the needs of all of the people involved. From that vantage point, the arrogance of vengeance and self-righteous indignation will be viewed as trapping the family in wasted emotional energy which severely limits its ability to achieve goals such as preparing individuals to function effectively and happily in a rapidly changing world. The strife, bitterness, and egocentrism which has traditionally wreaked emotional havoc in the stepfamilies of the past can then be more easily discarded and replaced with caring, humility, maturity, adaptability, love and joy.

The answers we have formulated for the questions which are included in *Remarried With Children* imply the presence of, and are intended to encourage the development of, a *learning family* mentality in stepfamilies.

The Past: It is history. Make the present good and the past will take care of itself.

--Author Unknown

Q:

How do I introduce my stepparent? What name could I use?

A:

Introductions are a social courtesy which are meant to put people at ease. Some children feel shy about introducing a stepparent and avoid it altogether, which really doesn't solve the problem. It is a good idea to discuss this with your parent and stepparent so that each of you may better understand one another's feeling. The challenge is to decide what is most comfortable for you while still considering your stepparent's feelings.

Becoming comfortable about introducing your stepparent is sometimes a matter of practice. You may need to try out different ways, over a period of time, to see what feels most comfortable for you. It might be, "This is my stepdad," or "This is George." You might want to use one way of introducing your stepparent with your friends and another way with your family. Whatever it is, you will know when you find the name that works best, and you will feel more at ease as time goes on.

Friends in your life are like the pillars on your porch.
Sometimes they hold you up, and sometimes they lean on you.
Sometimes it's just enough to know they are standing by.

—Author Unknown

Q:

I feel mixed-up when I have fun with my stepparent because my real parent, who does not live with me, does not like my stepparent. Is it okay for me to have fun with my stepparent?

A:

You can love your parent <u>and</u> enjoy your stepparent. It is not up to you to make the parents in your life like each other. When they don't get along with each other, it makes things hard for you. Whenever possible, you can tell them, or another trusted adult, how you feel. It may help you to think of your stepparent as an adult who is your friend, or thinking of your stepparent as you would an aunt or an uncle. You have the right to enjoy each adult in your life in your own way, whether or not your parents approve of it.

If you have never been hated by your child,
you've never been a parent.

—Bette Davis

Is there something wrong if I don't like my stepparent?

Sometimes stepchildren find it hard to like a stepparent. Although it is not very comfortable, it is not "wrong." It can be difficult to accept a stepparent who may be a stranger at first.

Relationships are a "two-way-street"; they take time to develop, and both people have to be willing to work at it. Some stepparents may be unsure about how to relate to children. Your stepparent may be having a hard time just as you are.

It may be helpful to ask your parent what he or she likes about your stepparent. This can give you a different way of thinking about your stepparent. Give yourself and your stepparent a chance.

Love seems the swiftest, but it is the slowest of all growths. No man or woman really knows what perfect love is until they have been married a quarter of a century.

--Mark Twain

Q:

I am confused. Before our marriage I felt ready to accept my role as a stepparent. Now, some months into the marriage, I feel very awkward, resentful, and uncomfortable about parenting my stepchildren. Is this to be expected?

A:

Your dilemma is very familiar. Your feelings are among the most typical feelings for new stepparents. These feelings are not a reflection of you personally. They are your reaction to what is actually happening as compared with what you thought would happen in your relationship with your stepchildren. One of the most often-heard reactions of stepparents is that the reality of stepfamily life is more complex than they had ever imagined.

In addition, you may feel that some things are happening too quickly while other things don't seem to happen fast enough. Perhaps you are expecting too much too soon of yourself and others. Step relationships are not as automatic as birth relationships and require time, respectful attention, extra patience, and cooperation in order to become positive and effective.

It's not what you know when you start.
It's what you learn and put to good use.

--Author Unknown

Q:

I have a problem with my stepmother and would like to talk about it with my father. I feel uncomfortable bringing this up. How can I talk with him?

A:

Bringing this up with your father may be hard, and yet, it is important for you to discuss these things with him. You could say, "I'm having a problem with (my step-mother). I don't want to hurt your feelings, and I need to talk about this." Let him know that you need his help.

If he has a hard time with what you are telling him, remember that your feelings are still important. You may not be able to solve everything with one discussion. Be willing to come back and talk about it again. In the meantime, you may find it helpful to talk about the situation with another adult such as a trusted teacher or school counselor.

A family is a unit composed not only of children but of men, women, an occasional animal, and the common cold.

–Ogden Nash

Q:

As a stepparent, which loyalty has the higher priority: my relationship with my spouse, or his relationship to his children?

A:

During one of our stepfamily discussion groups, a father used a good analogy. He told us that he was concerned that his spouse (the stepparent) sometimes feels like she is a "contract-laborer" in a company (the stepfamily) in which his biological children are the "regular employees." His wife felt that she was expendable in this enterprise, since "contract-laborers" would be the first to be let go by a company. His children, on the other hand, were seen as permanent employees with seniority in this company (the stepfamily).

Neither loyalty need be more important than the other. They are different relationships with different loyalties. Each needs room to grow. The existing bonds between birth parents and their children need to be respected because they have existed longer, and in some ways, may even be stronger than a new spousal relationship.

One of the important reasons for marrying is that we can look forward to growing in love over the years, remaining emotionally and physically together. Conversely, parent-child relationships are the ones that, in the normal course of events, experience separation, physically moving apart, when the children become adults. Because, almost always, all parties to a stepfamily have experienced separation and the emotional pain that goes with it, it is not uncommon for them to become sensitive to fears of abandonment. These fears can be triggered when loyalties are divided. It is important to take the time to give reassurance to everyone--by words and actions--of the strength of the commitment to them. Time and attention paid to one or the other is NOT an abandonment; no one is going to be "fired" from this corporation!

An existing parent-child relationship may have a head start on a new marriage, yet a marriage is different--not a competing relationship. You need to find ways to promote the healthy growth of each of these relationships.

A spoonful of honey will catch more flies than a gallon of vinegar.

—Benjamin Franklin

Q:

Do I need to obey my stepfather when my mother is not at home?

**A:**

When children talk to us about whether or not they should obey a stepparent, it usually turns out that they are having a lot of angry and sad feelings over the many changes in their lives. Disobeying may be a way that you are working out your feelings and it usually doesn't solve anything.

You may not feel much like cooperating now, but successful families require a lot of cooperation with others and consideration of their feelings. With the exception of something that your stepfather asks you to do that you know is wrong, it is best to cooperate.

If you are having problems with the way you are being treated by your stepfather, it is important to bring this up with your mother. Talking with her may open the door for discussion that could be helpful to the whole family.

Children are a great comfort in your old age -
and they help you to reach it faster, too

—Lionel M. Kauffman

My husband and I have been living with his two children since we married three years ago. Now, two more of his children have come to live with us. Even though I had agreed to this move because it was so important to my husband, I now feel overwhelmed. How do I handle myself in the family?

The prevailing reality is that stepfamilies have to function as much, if not more, in a child-centered way than do biological families. At this point it is very important that you and your spouse talk about all of your feelings and reactions. It is better to get out all of your concerns, fears, and anger that sit on these things. (For example, you may have to take care of his children and not be able to take care of your own children, who are somewhere else.) It is not unusual to be emotionally divided. But it is now also important to PLAN how you will handle a variety of situations such as shared space among siblings, rivalries, behavior problems, the energy drain, chores and housework, etc.

Your couple relationship will be the cornerstone for all future adjustments. Flexibility and adaptability are two of the keys to a stepparent's successful emotional adjustment. Flexibility includes openness to change and a cooperative manner. Adaptability means a willingness to assume whatever "stances" and roles that are helpful to the children. On the other hand, an overzealous commitment or responsibility for new stepchildren can create negative reactions later, when stepchildren resist such pressure by stepparents. If you view this as an adventure and experiment in family living rather than as an involuntary servitude, you will find it easier.

Say "yes" to the seedlings and a giant forest cleaves the sky.
Say "yes" to the universe and the planets become your neighbors.
Say "yes" to dreams of love and freedom. It is the password to utopia.

—Brooks Atkinson

Q:

I would like to invite my father, who does not live with me, to a school event, but I know my mother and stepfather would not like the idea. Do I invite him anyway?

A:

To want your parents to attend your school functions is natural. If your parents are at war with each other, even after the divorce, it is very unpleasant for you and leaves you with a difficult decision. If your mother would clearly explain her objection to you, then you could consider it, but we believe the decision is up to you.

Observe the postage stamp; its usefulness depends upon its ability to stick to one thing until it gets there. Don't give up.

—Author Unknown

Q:

We have been a stepfamily for three years and it seems like we are not coming together as a family. How long does it take people in stepfamilies to get used to each other?

A:

The growth of a stepfamily is a long-term process. Research on stepfamilies shows that it takes an average of five-to-seven years to establish comfortable family relationships.

Stepfamilies go through stages of development. Researchers Elizabeth Einstein and Linda Albert refer to these stages as *fantasy, confusion, chaos, stability,* and *commitment.* The stages vary in length. The *fantasy* period, for example, is the initial period when expectations are idealistic; it may last from six months to several years. The other stages are about attempts to adjust to the awareness that the stepfamily has taken over the daily living functions of the original biological family. *Commitment,* the final stage, comes much later, once the family has successfully tested and tried itself.

The growth of healthy, loving relationships takes time and effort. Often, it seems as if there isn't enough time, and you are just getting started, when the children leave home to find their independence. If you have teenagers, they will probably be leaving home for college, military service, or jobs before everything feels "great." It is difficult to motivate all parties involved to expend the needed effort during what time there is. Some stepfamilies have decided to consider the making of a comfortable blended family a lifetime project. We are inclined to agree.

The mind is like a parachute. It only works when it's open.

—Author Unknown

Q:

What do I call my stepgrandparents and aunts/uncles?

A:

Think about what you would like to call these family members and trust your feelings. Talking with your parents and friends about this may help you decide.

Your stepgrandparents, step-uncles and aunts may have some suggestions for you, too. If you are not comfortable with these suggestions, find a time alone with each person and maybe the two of you can work this out together.

Children need love, especially when they do not deserve it.

—Harold S. Hubert

Q:

Can I have the same kind of relationship with my stepchild as with my birth child?

A:

Expecting step relationships and birth relationships to be *exactly* the same is unrealistic, and bound to lead to disappointment. The majority of parents we have worked with over the years report that the relationships are definitely different. Step relationships can become very close and loving, but they are not meant to replace the birth parent relationship. In fact, it is not necessary that the *feelings* be the same in both step and biological relationships.

Your *role* in both relationships is essentially the same--a responsible, caring, non-shaming adult. If you can develop an appreciation of the differences, your step relationship will be effective and enjoyable.

Because it is common sense
doesn't mean it is common practice.

—Author Unknown

My mother talks badly about my father, who is not living with us. Do I speak up to defend him?

This can be a confusing situation for you. You may feel that you are being put in the middle and are being asked to take sides. It sounds like ignoring what is said is not working for you. You are being bothered by a problem which can be solved only by your parents.

No matter how old you are, it is painful to hear someone say something bad about someone you love. What you can do is tell your mother how you feel. Ask her not to say those things around you.

Insomnia: a contagious disease often transmitted
from babies to parents.

— Shannon Fife

Q:

My stepchild ignores, discounts, and rejects me as a parent figure. What are some of the reasons children are reluctant to open the door for stepparents?

A:

It really hurts to be shut out by the children when you are ready to offer them emotional and financial support.

It takes some children a long time to accept the fact that their birth parents are not going to get back together. The child may imagine that you are the barrier to the parent reunion they wish for. They hold off their stepparents while they hold out hope. As a result, you get their misplaced anger and blame.

In addition, your stepchildren may be confused about their loyalties, believing that if they listen to you, they are betraying or hurting their birth parent. In a bitter post-divorce situation, for example, angry and self-pitying parents sometimes encourage children to feel guilty about allegiances. It takes time, maturity, and an understanding environment for the children to figure out how to happily fit you into their lives.

Families break up when people take hints you don't intend and miss hints that you do intend.

--Robert Frost

Q:

My mother has remarried and is planning to move. This will take me away from my father, and I don't want to go. What can I do?

A:

Speak up! It is very important for your opinions and feelings to be considered. You have a right to be a part of both your parents' lives. In many cases, children are moved away from one of their parents by the other parent, who is trying to make the best decisions for him/herself and his/her children as he/she makes a new life. However, if this means seeing your other parent less often, it is very important that your feelings on the matter be heard.

If the move cannot be stopped, be sure you know what arrangements have been made for communication and visitation with your father or mother.

My mother loved children - she would have given anything
if I had been one.

--Groucho Marx

Q:

As parents in a new stepfamily, can we expect to be able to discipline each other's children?

A:

A stepparent's ability to play an effective role in parental discipline is dependent on several factors. How much time you have spent with this child, how well you get along with this child, and how much emotional support you receive from your spouse, are some considerations. Also, how much acrimony and competition exists between yourself and your spouse's "ex" will be important. It is prudent to take on the disciplining of one another's child gradually. Initially, the birthparent may need to handle much of the discipline. Stepparents need time to get to know the children before effective discipline can occur. Your credibility--as an advisor and guide--will not be taken for granted by the children. You earn this status over time. Effective discipline rests on a foundation of mutual respect between yourself and this child. You will also need the support of your spouse in order to exercise parental discipline effectively. Spouses legitimize each other's parental role in the child's eyes.

The Golden Rule of Friendship and Communication--
Listen to others as you would have them listen to you.

--Author Unknown

I have been angry since my father remarried. How can I stop being so angry?

A certain amount of anger is okay. It can even be positive. Anger is the feeling we use to help us do what we need to do to protect ourselves. If you have too little anger, people will be able, more easily, to take advantage of you. If you have too much anger, you will probably do something destructive. If your anger lasts too long, it can take away from energy which you need in order to be productive in other things, like school.

Think about why you're really angry and who you're really angry with. We may feel angry when we lose things that are very important to us: money, personal possessions, loved ones, the family we once knew. We feel frustrated and angry when we have no power to keep it from happening. We feel angry when we feel unprotected.

The challenge is to get the anger out without harming anyone. Your anger will not change what has happened, but getting your anger out will help you feel better. Find ways to let this anger out, such as playing sports, taking walks, kicking cardboard boxes, or talking about it with a friend or counselor.

Experience is a hard teacher because she gives the test first, and teaches the lesson afterwards.

--Vernon Law

Q:

As a stepparent, can I have the same *expectations* of stepchildren as I do my birthchildren?

A:

Unrealistic expectations are the single greatest bugaboo for stepfamilies. In any situation, disappointment is greatest when expectations are high compared to the actual outcome. In other words, if you expect more of your stepchildren than can reasonably be obtained, you both will be disappointed.

There is a tendency in stepparents to expect the same kinds of respect, affection, and obedience from stepchildren as from biological children. We encourage you to treat each of your children and your stepchildren as a unique individual, and set your expectations accordingly. Get to know each one's strengths and weaknesses, understand their personal history--of losses, disappointments, successes, and failures--and take into account their maturity and their motivations. You need to clearly state your expectations, and set them at a level which will insure the children's success.

Remember that your stepchildren will have expectations of you, too. What basis would you like for them to use in setting those expectations?

Everyday comes bearing its gifts--untie the ribbons.

--Ann Ruth Schabacker

Q:

I'm sad a lot since my mother has remarried. How can I stop being sad?

A:

Sadness is the feeling that happens naturally when we lose something. Sadness is natural for children when parents marry again. You've lost the way the family was when your parents were married to each other, and that hurts. It will take time to feel better.

Certain things which we see and hear make us feel sad, because they remind us of something we had but don't have now. When you see that your mother is happy with her new husband, it reminds you that you no longer have both parents together. You are sad. Holidays and birthdays can also make children sad as they remember the "good old days." When you spend Thanksgiving or other holidays at two homes, you are reminded of a time when there was only one home. This kind of sadness may never completely go away, but it will be less strong as time goes on.

In automobile terms, the child supplies the power but the parents have to do the steering.

--Benjamin Spock

Q:

Can a stepparent ever replace a birthparent for a child?

A:

Replacement is a strong concept. Stepparents who try to replace birthparents encounter serious problems with stepchildren and within themselves. Therefore, we prefer to talk about the *influence* of parents. A stepparent cannot replace the *genetic* influence of a birthparent. However, under certain conditions, a stepparent may have a more significant *psychological* influence than a birthparent on the personality development of a child.

There are very important roles which a stepparent can fulfill for a stepchild: mentor, friend, counselor, and advisor. You can consider it a victory if your stepchildren come to accept you as a caring adult who gives good advice. To succeed as a stepparent it is not necessary for you to actually become another traditional "parent."

On a day-to-day basis, a stepparent may provide many things for a stepchild which could also be provided by a birthparent. Often, stepparents feel a "step away" from being a full-fledged parent because their influence may not be evident in the short run. Many years may pass before children have the maturity or willingness to let you know how much of a positive influence you have been.

You are the bows from which your children,
as living arrows, are sent forth.

--Kahlil Gibran

Q:

My mother is talking seriously about remarrying. If this happens, I will have a stepfamily which I don't think I want in the first place. The worst part is that I will be forced to share my room and things with my new stepbrother. What can I do?

A:

This is a big change and it may be hard to accept. Keep in mind that your stepbrother will probably be going through the same kind of things you are: you will both have to make room for each other. This may not be as bad as you think: your stepbrother may have some neat things to share with you! Sharing and cooperating rather than avoiding each other will probably make your life more peaceful; yet, sharing and cooperating with someone who you did not particularly choose, is an enormous challenge. You will have an even bigger adjustment if you are not used to sharing with other brothers and sisters.

Your attitude, how you look at the coming events, will make a big difference in how things work out. Are you ready to look at your stepbrother as a brother, or at least, as a potential friend and ally, rather than an alien who has invaded your family?

We recommend lots of talking about the coming changes ahead of time with all family members. Two important steps for you to take are:
   * talk about the changes privately with your own parent;
   * talk privately to your stepbrother-to-be about how you will work out the sharing.

No matter how much you talk about the changes ahead of time, some things will come up later that you couldn't anticipate. To help deal with this, some families set up an agreement for family meetings to help settle differences. We think family meetings are a good idea.

The gem cannot be polished without friction
nor people perfected without trials.

--Confucius

Q:

I am worried that the attention I give to my stepchildren deprives my own children of attention that they need.

A:

Although the capacity for love and affection is great, many parents experience a virtuous concern as to whether or not it is possible to treat all of your children "the same." From time to time, one child may need and get more attention, time, money, or whatever, than the others. However, if there is inconsistency or an imbalance of attention which lasts too long, there will be trouble. When the factor of attention is out of balance--just as in balancing the tires on your car--some family members will feel as if they are getting more wear and tear than others. It is a good idea to "rotate" your attention periodically to reduce the likelihood of having an emotional blow-out.

In situations such as in new stepfamilies, one or another of the children is likely to feel alienated, lonely, or left out at some time. It is appropriate, then, to increase or shift your attention accordingly. It is important to talk to your spouse and the children about why you are giving someone special attention. (P.S. *You* or *your spouse* might be the one in need of that special attention, as we all are from time to time.)

It's very depressing the first time you realize you have
a cat that answers to "Kitty",
dog that answers to "Rover",
and three kids who answer to nobody.

--Robert Orben

Q:

My stepchild has made a number of negative comments based on his observations of his father. As his stepfather, how do I handle this negative information about a child's non-custodial or absent parent?

A:

One parent told us that when the children brought negative comments, criticisms, or observations about their non-custodial parent, she wished she were deaf and didn't have to hear them. She was very uncomfortable. When this happens to you, it is time to go into a special state of mind called "L.W.J." --Listening Without Judging. This means:

1. Listen *carefully*--there may be truth in what you are being told; there may be exaggeration; there are surely *feelings* behind the words.
2. Ask questions such as, "How can I help?" "What would you like to do about that?" and "What could have made him/her act that way?"
3. Show appreciation for the feelings involved.
4. Do not join the bad-mouthing, blaming, or criticizing.
5. Do not automatically assume that the child is wrong and the other adult is right.
6. Let the child know that he has a right to his opinions and feelings so he can learn to trust himself.

7. Advocate for the child whenever it is appropriate.
8. Keep the information confidential whenever possible. Exceptions are when you need to discuss something with your spouse, for example, or when you suspect that abuse has occurred. Let the child know whether or not you intend to keep information confidential.

Children have never been very good at listening to their elders, but they have never failed to imitate them.

--James Baldwin

Q:

I feel as though my mother pays too much attention to my new stepfather. How do I get my mother's attention?

A:

If it seems that your mother is paying a lot of attention to your stepfather at the beginning of their marriage, you may be right. It is not unusual to feel jealous about this. It also could be that your mother is still giving you attention, but you are not used to sharing her with someone else. Ask your mother for time alone, and give her some specific suggestions of how to spend that time together. After a while you will find that you can have enough of your mother's attention even while you share her with the rest of the family.

A certain amount of opposition is a great help to people. Kites rise against, not with, the wind.

--John Neal

Q:

Are there special issues for teenagers in stepfamilies?

A:

Stepfamily formation will certainly, for a time, complicate the already distressing developmental period of adolescence. Teenagers typically experience stormy feelings and relationships during this period which usually lasts from one to five years. The adjustments required by divorce and remarriage add complications to this difficult period. The problems for children in their teens--and beyond--are related to the heightened awareness of what is happening to them. They also have a much better ability, than do the younger children, to articulate and demonstrate (act out) their uncertainties, fears, and discomforts. Some of the extra complications include:

- Children--especially teens--who are aware that their parents were hurt by the divorce may want to protect their parents. Often this means wanting to protect *both* parents at the same time and wanting relief for their own hurt. All of this can add up to serious inner conflict.
- Some teens may use extreme manipulations to protest a parent's remarriage, such as running away or deliberately provoking arguments.
- Some become depressed, lose their appetites, or have trouble sleeping.

- Feelings may intensify: anger, loss, fear, feeling misunderstood, wanting to be alone.

Strong feelings can emerge from teenagers as they adjust to stepfamily life. These emotions usually subside with understanding, time, and the realization that they and their parents are healing and recovering from the trauma of divorce and remarriage.

The best way to keep children at home is to make
the home atmosphere pleasant,
and let the air out of the tires.

--Dorothy Parker

Q:

My mother is paying much more attention to my stepsister than me. I don't undestand why. Am I not as important anymore?

A:

You are still important. You are just as important as you were before your stepfamily was formed. Perhaps your stepsister needs more effort from your mother to make their relationship okay. Your mother may enjoy the fact that she can depend upon your relationship enough that she can give more attention to another child in the family.

It will help to let your mother know how you feel. An example of what you might say is, "Mom, when you are giving your attention to Susan (stepsister), I feel left out. Will you spend more time with me, please?"

The real menace in dealing with a five-year-old is that in no time at all you begin to sound like a five-year-old.

--Joan Kerr

Q:

How do we decide what a child will call a stepparent?

A:

We recommend encouraging a child to decide what he or she will call a stepparent. It is better to promote comfort for a child by allowing some exploration and experimentation with names. An older child may have a problem referring to a stepparent by any name. Talking this over openly is a good idea.

Brainstorming to come up with a comfortable name such as Dad-Bill, Pop, Papa, Bill, or any variation of the name referring to the father can help. (For younger children, this can be made into a game.) Flexibility on the part of the adults will go a long way toward finding a satisfactory solution to this common stepfamily challenge.

What counts in making a happy marriage
is not so much how compatible you are,
but how you deal with incompatibility.

--George Levinger

Q:

My mother has married again and I don't want to be at home. I feel like going to live with my father who is still single. What do I do?

 A:

It is not unusual that you feel this way about your new family. It is our experience that many children feel this way. Often these feelings are temporary and, after a period of adjustment, most children do not make the move to live with their other parent.

Your feelings are important. It will help for you to let both of your parents know how you feel. Perhaps they can help you figure out why you are unhappy, and help you come up with some solutions. Talking to friends and other trusted adults may help, too. If your feelings do not ease up in three-to-six months, we would suggest family counseling to help you make the best decision.

To keep your marriage brimming
With love in the loving cup,
Whenever you're wrong admit it;
Whenever you're right shut up.

--Ogden Nash

Q:

Is it helpful for a birthparent to be a mediator between a stepparent and a stepchild? Sometimes I feel as if I am caught in the crossfire. I'm only trying to help and they both turn on me!

 **A:**

Whenever possible, a stepparent needs to manage his or her own relationship with a stepchild.

The word "mediate" comes from words meaning "to be in the middle." In the most positive sense, you get in the middle of an argument to help settle it. If you jump in and start mediating without being asked to do so, then you are meddling. The parties involved may rightly ask you to mind your own business. If that is the case, then it is no wonder you feel as if you are getting it from both sides.

In order for mediation to work, it will probably be necessary for you to ask both parties to accept you in that role. If the parties involved do not want you to get involved, then leave the room, take a walk--get out of their way--and realize the risk you run by interfering.

You have an opinion and you have a right to express it. However, when there are conflicts between others, you may be better off taking your opinions to each person privately. That way, in a more neutral atmosphere, others can be more receptive to your support and your suggestions.

I have found the best way to give advice to your children is to find out what they want and then advise them to do it.

--Harry S. Truman

Q:

I have lived with my father for several years. Since he remarried, I feel more like I have a whole family again. Now, I don't feel like visiting my mother--who is single--anymore. Do I ask to stop visiting? (age 12)

A:

Keep visiting. You once thought of your family as being you and your mother and father. "Families" can be much more than that. You are faced with the challenge of being part of what is called an "extended" family. Like a tree with branches that grow out in many directions, your family is growing, too. All of the branches are part of the tree.

You are excited about having a stepfamily, and wanting to spend more time with them is understandable. However, your visits to your mother are still very important. Your mother is, and always will be, part of your family. One of the miracles of life is that, no matter how big a family grows to be, there is enough love for everyone.

Poise is the art of raising the eyebrows instead of the roof.

--Author Unknown

Q:

How do we handle verbal abuse from a child to a stepparent?

A:

Anger is to be expected in any family. It is the role of the parents and other responsible adults to make clear--by explanation and example--the difference between anger which serves the role of self-protection, and anger which has harmful consequences to others. We all have a right to protect ourselves and express ourselves, but that right ends if, in the process, harmful consequences come to others. The concept of protecting without harming needs to be explained without shaming the child.

Abusive language usually takes one of several forms. The abuse may involve belittling one's thoughts, feelings, or one's sexuality, or disparaging one's morality, intentions, or integrity. All abuse involves shaming and must be avoided. Therefore, it is important to establish a mutual agreement not to verbally abuse.

Make sure you are specific about what you mean by verbal abuse. For example, saying "no" is not the same as name-calling. Stepchildren use a variety of means to avoid facing the reality of the existence of the authority--which may be newly vested--of the stepparent. Ignoring, "tuning out," doing what is expected but not talking, leaving the house rather than obeying are also ways that children rebuff stepparents. These resistances may indicate a lack of readiness to function in a parent-child way. Verbal abuse often arises out of the judgmental attitudes and defenses experienced in earlier relationships. What feels like verbal abuse from a child to stepparent may really be a symptom of a breakdown in the relationship between that child and one or both of his natural parents. Interpreting to a child the possible causes of verbal abuse can help that child gain insight into why he is doing it and provides motivation for establishing greater control over it. Verbal abuse by a stepparent to a child needs to be stopped and examined immediately.

To make your children capable of honesty
is the beginning of education.

--John Ruskin

Q:

Because of joint custody, I am going back and forth between my mom's and dad's homes just about every other week. Is it okay to ask if I can make one place my home and the other a place to visit? (age 10)

A:

Ask for what you want. Some children have told us that, even after trying to live with your kind of joint custody arrangement, they find that it is more comfortable and more practical to live in one place, and visit the other. Talk to your parents about it, together, if possible. Let them know your reasons and that you love them both.

You can love both of your parents even if you live in one home and visit the other. Where you live does not determine how much you love. Being settled into one home can help you feel more relaxed about things like schoolwork and making friends. You have a right to live in one place most of the time, if that makes you happier.

Diplomacy is the art of putting your foot down without stepping on anybody's toes.

--Franklin P. Jones

Q:

I want my husband (a stepparent) to be involved in the discipline of my children and yet, I'm uncomfortable when he is. How do I deal with my conflicting feelings?

A:

Express your feelings to your husband. Nervousness, worry, uncertainty, and anger are not unusual when it comes to issues of discipline. After all, you may have handled things alone just fine for years. You will probably need many discussions with your spouse in order to arrive at mutual agreement on child-rearing and discipline.

Once your husband and the children get to know each other, and have developed a relationship of their own, it is important for you to let go of some of the power. You may find that asking your spouse to handle some of the smaller things at first will help you and the children to feel comfortable sharing this parental responsibility. Gradually, you will feel more comfortable turning over control on some of the more important issues.

You may find that physically removing yourself from the room, as your spouse handles things, will help you stay out of it. It is important to support your spouse's decisions as much as possible if you are going to be consistent. Reversing your spouse's judgments can become a destructive pattern for your children. With time and practice you will feel more comfortable relying on your spouse.

The family you came from isn't as important as the family you're going to have.

--Ring Lardner

Q:

Since my mother married again, my father has stopped seeing me or slowed down visits. What can I do?

A:

This sometimes happens and it can feel like a terrible rejection. If you can, ask him why he is not seeing you, and tell him how you feel. Adults sometimes become very confused about what they should do. Let him know that, even though you now have a stepfather, you would like your own father to be just as close, and in touch, as ever. Remember that whatever he decides to do, it is not your fault. You are still a lovable child whether he sees you or not.

Anyone who thinks he knows all the answers
isn't up-to-date on the questions.

--Frank Lawrence

Q:

We are a remarried couple with children from previous marriages. Will having a child of our own help our stepfamily?

A:

It is important to understand that the life cycle and development pattern of a stepfamily--which adds members of different ages at different times--is quite different from the formation of a traditional, biological family--which adds members one-at-a-time through a pregnancy and birthing process, starting "from scratch." Adding an "ours" baby creates still another type of family, one which we are just beginning to understand and which no one knows exactly how to manage. While there is some evidence that an "ours" baby may help re-center the family and bring people closer together, having a baby in the early years may not be as helpful. There is no single activity, event, situation, or condition--such as having a baby--that will solve the problem of how to make your stepfamily feel comfortable, loving, and free of conflict. Finding comfort, discovering how you can live together, and learning to feel like a family will be the result of a "mix" of activities, events, and efforts.

After all, what is a pedestrian? He is a man who has
two cars - one being driven by his wife,
the other by one of his children.

--Robert Bradbury

Q:

We are a stepfamily with a child visiting us part of the time. My husband abandons everyone and everything to be with his child during the visit. How do I deal with the frustrations that this creates for me as a stepparent?

A:

The key here is balance. It is helpful to view this problem within the larger scope of your stepfamily life together. Your resentment of the time he spends with his children may really be a problem of not having enough time as a couple or it may bring to mind problems that you have with his children. Try to solve each problem separately. Dealing with problems one at a time is one of the most effective ways to resolve conflict.

Your husband is experiencing a typical problem. He misses his children a great deal and, when they visit, he tries to make up for lost time or lost opportunities. The fact that he is capable of such feelings is quite positive. Objecting will probably make things harder for both of you.

Talk it over with him and ask that you be a part of their time together, some of the time, without imposing yourself. Encourage him to find a balance between his time alone

111

with his children and the time he needs to spend with others. Stepparents also report that there are benefits from having alone time with the stepchildren.

Considering the competing interests and demands of stepfamily life, many couples need to negotiate couple time, too, entirely apart from the children.

No one ever injured his eyesight
by looking on the bright side of things.

--Author Unknown

Q:

Since my dad remarried, I am expected to eat certain foods, follow new rules, and participate in activities with my new family. I don't like any of it. Is there a way to escape all of this?

A:

Complete escape is probably not an option. You do have a right to your opinions, and letting your parents know how you feel about things is very important. Speaking up about which foods and activities you would like--not only about those that you don't like--may help you get your point across. Getting to a comfortable arrangement often takes a great deal of "talking things out."

Change is not easy, especially if you are being asked to give up something that is familiar for something that is new and different--even when the new way is an improve-ment. In our experience, when new ways of doing things are forced on the family, it can create resentment which, sooner or later, makes things harder. We believe it is to the family's advantage to bring about most changes gradually, and to look for compromises which retain some of the familiar ways.

We also encourage family members to be open to new ways of doing things and to give the new ways a chance. We know of many instances in which a family member tried out something that was introduced to them by a stepparent or a stepchild and they not only liked it, they became enthusiastic about it.

I now perceive one immense omission in my psychology -
the deepest principle of human nature
is the craving to be appreciated.

--William James

Q:

My mom remarried and I miss my dad more than ever. Why do I feel this way? (age 8)

A:

There may be many reasons for your feelings. It is very typical, for example, that a remarriage tells you more definitely that your parents will not get back together. If this is true for you, you may feel sadness, or feel like you miss your father more.

You may find that during the time that you are getting used to your stepfather, you may miss you father more. Keep in mind that your stepfather has replaced your father in your mother's marriage, but your stepfather does not replace your father in your life.

If you can, talk about your feelings with your father or your mother. When you visit with your dad, remembering how much you have missed him can help you enjoy the time you spend with him even more.

If a child is to keep alive his inborn sense of wonder, he needs the companionship of at least one adult who can share it, rediscovering with him the joy, excitement and mystery of the world we live in.

--Rachel Carson

Q:

I am an involved, concerned stepparent. My husband's "ex"--the up-'til-now uninvolved birthparent--suddenly wants to be involved with the children's lives and achievements. What can I do?

A:

Interfering with the child's relationship with the birthparent can be a disaster.

Nancy Konesko, writing for Knight-Ridder Newspapers says, "The minute you marry a divorced man with children, you get a package deal--the man, his ex-wife, and their children." And, of course, it's just the reverse when you marry a woman with children and an ex-husband. Author Ann Cryster calls this "ex" the wife-in-law (or husband-in-law). She estimates there are 14 million American women (and how many men?) in these relationships "locking horns in endless rounds of jealousy and anger."

Your part in avoiding this trap is to be as tolerant and understanding as possible of your stepchildren, treat them well, treat them fairly.

Recognize that a child's connection to a birthparent is a strong bond, and needs to be respected, not attacked. The birthparent may have stepped out of the picture for a variety of reasons and without malicious intent. It is better not to resist this parent's involvement again. Dealing with an "ex" is less convenient and more complicated than if they had stayed out of the picture altogether. Accept that the bond exists and, if you have been there for your stepchild, she/he will know it. Acknowledge and honor whatever you have with your stepchild, do not abandon it. Be prepared to help your stepchild-- when asked--to discover what kind of relationship she/he needs from you and from her/ his birthparent.

A successful marriage requires falling in love many times, always with the same person.

--Mignon McLaughlin

Q:

My father has been through two marriages and divorces. I don't have faith that marriage can work. Is there hope for marriage?

 **A:**

Yes, there is hope. We are aware that divorce is so widespread in the United States that the prospect of marriage is becoming discouraging to some children. However, don't judge your father--or anybody else, for that matter--harshly just because he has been married more than once. Many people marry only once and it lasts a lifetime. Others find lasting happiness after one or more remarriages. Marriage can work. It seems that some people need to be married more than once to find out how to make it work successfully.

Seek out adults who are successful in marriage and talk to them about it. Some of your relatives and other adults (teachers, counselors, clergy) may be helpful in your understanding that marriage can be successful.

I looked on child-rearing not only as a work of love and duty but as a profession that was fully as interesting and challenging as any honorable profession in the world and one that demanded the best that I could bring it.

--Rose Kennedy

Q:

I do not feel love for my stepchild right now and I feel guilty. What's wrong?

A:

Feelings of parent-child love between a stepparent and stepchild are neither necesary nor sufficient for an effective step relationship. And they are not possible in some situations. Your willingness to be a responsible, caring adult, spending time, allowing the relationship to develop gradually will have a powerful influence.

Nothing need be wrong. With a birthchild there are a number of biological, psychological, and social factors at work to promote bonding. Not only are these supports absent for the most part in step relationships, there are real obstacles, too. You may feel like a "fifth wheel" at first, not having a clearly defined function, role, or purpose in the life of this child. Some "out of place" feeling is typical for new stepparents.

The formation of step relationships takes more time than most people realize. You can support your own patience by reminding yourself that the complicated dynamics of stepparent-child relationships frequently set up the stepparent to feel overly responsible, lost, and guilty. What is happening is not your fault. At various times, you may feel like an intruder or a victim, even when your motivation is to be helpful.

Your spouse's understanding and support will help you to accept the limitations of this new situation, and to develop the possibilities that lie within your step relationship. There are many opportunities for fun, love, good times, and strong, caring, rewarding relationships in the days and years ahead.

To love and be loved is to feel the sun from both sides.

--David Viscott

Q:

My younger sister and I have lived with our mother for twelve years since our parents divorced. Now, my sister has decided that she wants to live with my father. In a way, I would like to go, too, to be with her, and in another way, I don't want to leave my mother. How do I know what is best for me?

A:

You are torn because of your feelings for the people you love. You are facing changes and conflicts which probably were not anticipated at the time of the divorce because it is impossible to know ahead of time everything that will happen to us. Even when we have developed attitudes and habits of flexibility, negotiation, and compromise, there are difficult challenges.

What is best for you is to be honest about your feelings and have the family work with you to come up with a solution you all can live with. This usually means having lots of conversations, lots of compromises, and trying different approaches if the first one doesn't work out.

You haven't told us why your sister wants to move. She may need to do this for reasons which are hers alone, and your opinion does not have to be the same as her opinion. The fact that you feel conflict has something to do with the fact that you love your sister and your father and your mother. It will help from time to time to remember that your having strong feelings of love and loyalty is a strength.

The great secret of a successful marriage is to treat
all disasters as incidents and none of the incidents as disasters.

--Harold Nicholson

Q:

My spouse and I are so overwhelmed caring for our children and dealing with ex-spouses that we have little time or energy for us. What can we do about this?

A:

Quality time for the couple, apart from the children, is essential. It is your shock absorber for the bumps and jolts of stepfamily life. Some say it is the single most important factor in stepfamily survival. We recommend that couples set aside some special time for themselves at least every six weeks, and more often if possible. Put it on the calendar. Make it sacred time, not to be postponed. Enjoy looking forward to the time, and enjoy the time itself.

Meanwhile, make brief times during which you don't talk about the kids--not even a word. Create other ways of keeping in contact with each other: getting up fifteen minutes earlier together, calling each other at work, and doing household tasks together, e.g., grocery shopping, dinner, and laundry.

Join a stepparent support group. If one doesn't exist in your community, contact a church or mental health counselor and ask them to start a discussion group. Research shows that the stress of caregiving reduces the body's immune function and makes you less resistant to a variety of illnesses. The immune "suppression" was moderated or reversed for people who attended a support group.

Birthdays are our opportunity to give to kids all of the things they have given to us--but how do you gift-wrap high blood pressure?

--Robert Orben

Q:

I am a stepparent. My wife's ex-husband has stopped paying child support. I did not expect this and it has created serious financial problems. What are my obligations in this situation? How do we discuss this with the children?

A:

We are in an era during which many states are passing tougher laws to enforce payment of child support. Therefore, we might expect to see less of this problem in the future. You did not create the problem between your wife's ex-spouse and his children, yet you are affected by it. You do not have a legal obligation to replace child-support payments which have been ordered as part of a divorce decree. The decision to marry into the situation produces financial obligations related to your wife's debts.

You can support your stepchildren fully or you have the right to limit your monetary support. It is important to let your stepchildren know clearly the extent to which you can provide for them. We think it is best that the stepparent not get involved in trying to explain why the child's father has stopped paying child support. Stepchildren are better served when you tell them what you can and cannot do for them, so that they are not set up to be disappointed if you cannot do it.

This kind of situation--unresolved legal issues, lawyers, emotional upheaval, additional financial drain from fees, and time off from your job--can put extreme strain on a remarriage. Solutions are not easily or quickly found. You would be wise to consider investing in the services of a qualified counselor who can help you sort out your feelings, brainstorm creative solutions, maintain perspective, and keep the lines of communication open between you and your spouse.

He that will have his son have a respect for him and his orders must have a great reverence for his son.

--John Locke

Q:

I am a 14 year old boy and my mother has been remarried for as long as I can remember. I like my stepfather, but I would like to spend time with my real father who I have not seen in years. I do not know why he has not stayed in touch with me. How do I go about trying to contact him?

A:

You may have wondered what it would be like to live with your father. This is a common desire for young people who have not had much or any time with their fathers. Naturally, you want to find out more about an important person in your life.

Many boys think about spending more time with their fathers, and at about your age, they get up the nerve to say it out loud! We admire your courage to try to make such a visit happen. You want to know about your father, and it is hard for a young person to get an accurate picture of one parent from the other parent. It will help you to try to get some of your own answers.

Because your mother has legal custody of you, you will need her help (permission) to arrange this visit. Talk with your mother and stepfather about this. Most likely, your mother and stepfather will understand your need to see your father. If you are afraid that your father may not agree to see you, writing him a letter first could help pave the way for a visit. Maybe a telephone call could follow a letter. Your mother might volunteer to call for you so that your father knows that you have her support.

It is a good idea to talk over your expectations, hopes, worries and other feelings with your mother, stepfather, or someone outside the family. Plan to use their support both before and after your contact with your father.

Success in marriage does not come merely through
finding the right mate, but through being the right mate.

--Barnett Brickner

Q:

We have been living together to "try out" blending her children and mine before we actually marry. Can we expect that anything will really change after we are legally married?

A:

You can usually expect to see a mixture of changes in your social and emotional life as a family after you legally marry. You have gained some insight about one another by living together. Legalizing the marriage produces a social contract which normally has emotional consequences for your entire extended families. Marriage creates an official status for the stepfamily unit and new social interactions between new relatives.

Especially for children, a remarriage can bring to the surface "unfinished emotional business." Some of it is related to the grief of letting go of the previous family's existence. Even for couples who have lived together a long time, marriage can produce these reactions. If the children have been aware of the "living together" arrangement, they may have been holding back from making their complete adjustment, waiting to see if things would work out. Only after the marriage can you begin to encounter what everyone goes through as members of the extended family recognize and accept your stepfamily unit as part of the larger family circle. An "ex" may also react to your marriage in ways that create a ripple of emotional effect for the family.

It is not a bad thing that children should occasionally, and politely, put parents in their place.

--Colette

Q:

I am a 12 year old girl. My father has custody of me and he remarried when I was nine years old. My problem is that I hate my stepmother. All we are doing now is ignoring each other as much as possible. My father is unhappy with me about this. But I can't help what I feel. What can I do?

A:

You sound hurt and angry. We cannot tell from your description what is the basis for your feelings. Sometimes leftover feelings about the divorce and remarriage get directed toward stepparents who don't deserve it. This could be happening to you. Sometimes stepparents who are well-meaning can come on too strong and too quickly, and you may feel that you are being pushed around.

Whatever the reasons, a stand-off in which you ignore each other may make you feel better but it will not help the situation to get better. Often, when we get into these stand-offs it is because we would really like to have a better relationship with that person, but we are hurt. Also, we may not realize that our actions have hurt the other person, too. Someone needs to say "I'm sorry, let's try again." That someone could be you.

There isn't a family we know of in which somebody doesn't get mad at somebody else once in a while and feels like not ever talking to that person again. But these things always seem to blow over as we live and work together and feel the love and support in the family. It is a sign of maturity to recognize that any of us can be pretty stubborn even when it isn't in our own best interest. Time and again we make peace with each other and get past our squabbles and back to the business of being a caring and forgiving family.

Before I got married I had six theories about bringing up children; now I have six children and no theories.

--John Wilmot, Lord Rochester

My ex-spouse is still angry about our divorce two years ago and, now that I have recently remarried, she has become more bitter. She has put me down when she talks to our children, and she has been critical of my new wife to the children, as well. The children are hurt and confused by all of this. What can I do?

This is a sad situation for everyone. It is sometimes tempting to try to change your ex-spouse. Telling her what she should and should not do will only make things worse. Part of the problem is that your "ex" has not yet emotionally divorced from you, and she needs more time to do this. She may interpret any discussion of the children--or custody or finances--as another chance to win you back or to keep hope alive. It is important not to give "mixed" messages to her when discussing the children. Be clear that these discussions are for the children, not for her or you.

Remember that any attack by you can keep you and her connected in an emotionally unhealthy way. Work on using anger for the purpose of establishing the limits of the relationship, as a protection for your new family. This is very different from being angry against her.

Be assertive and persistent. Assertiveness may require you to repeat things several times to make your point clear and understood.

Children grow up emotionally healthy--become effective and joyful adults--when they receive effective parenting. Effective parenting acknowledges the value, vulnerability, imperfection, dependence, and immaturity of the child and treats those conditions with non-shaming respect. Effective parents provide a non-abusive structure out of which the child grows to effective adulthood. When one parent belittles the other, the child feels shame. Instilling this kind of feeling on a child whose emotional defenses are not fully developed--and therefore cannot resist--is a form of abuse.

If your "ex" is being emotionally abusive to the children, you must intervene to stop it. And you can still help the children grow through the conflict. If this has continued for any length of time, the children may appreciate professional mental health counseling to assist them in dealing with their feelings.

You also have the positive help of your new spouse who, if she can step back and be a supportive listener for the children, and not become embroiled in the jealousy, can do the children a world of good. Help your children talk about and understand their feelings and come to their own conclusions. With help, your children can figure all this out; help them as much as they let you!

We must have a place where children can have
a whole group of adults they can trust.

--Margaret Mead

Q:

I am a nine year old boy. My dad got married again about two years ago. His wife, my stepmother, bugs me about every little thing--how I eat my food, how I talk and how I keep my room. I get so mad at her I don't know what to do. How can I get her to stop doing these things?

A:

It is not easy to accept a stepparent who takes over things that your mom is supposed to do.

If you can't talk to your stepmother about how you feel, it is important to let your dad know. Sometimes stepmothers want to be mothers because they 1) want to help their husbands with their children and they 2) want to do things with stepchildren which they feel that the children's mother has not done as well. Sometimes stepmothers come in and take over the care of the children, because the fathers want them to. We can understand why you are mad at your stepmother for telling you what to do. If your dad agrees with how your stepmother deals with you, then your problem is really with your dad. If your dad disagrees with how your stepmother deals with you, then you need help from your dad about how to handle yourself.

ASTOUNDING STATISTICS[*]

* 70 million Americans, in one way or another, are involved in stepfamilies.[1]

* By 1990, more people were part of a second marriage than a first.[1]

* 1 out of 3 children live in some form of a step relationship.[3]

* 4 million people become available for remarriage every year . . . and the ensuing stepfamily.[4]

* A half million couples with children remarry every year.[4]

* 84% of divorced men and 75% of divorced women remarry within four years; 60% have children.[2]

* One out of every 6 (7 million) children, lives in a stepfamily.

* There are approximately 11 million children of divorce in this country.[2]

* 45% of children born today will live in a divorced family by age 18.[3]

* 35% of children born today will live in a stepfamily before they are 18.[3]

* Divorce is as upsetting and deleterious for children from affluent homes or for those whose parents are highly educated as it is for less advantaged children.[5]

* The average marriage in the United States lasts only seven years.[4]

* In 1930, one out of 50 couples were divorced. Now, 57% of all marriages end in divorce.[4]

Data Sources

[1]   Stepfamily Foundation, Inc., research and data.

[2]   ABC News Closeup: "After the Sexual Revolution," July 30, 1986, Show #127, hosted by Peter Jennings.

[3]   *USA Today* Newspaper, March 6, 1986. Janis Johnson, writer.

[4]   United States Bureau of Census, 1980 Census.

[5]   Kent University Study, John Guidubaldi, Ph.D., Professor of Early Childhood.

[·]   Adapted from "Stepfamily Foundation Statistics: The Numbers Tell the Story."

RESOURCES

The following resources to help your stepfamily are available through the STEP UP program at Ohio Professional Counseling Services, Inc., 3400 N. High Street, Suite 120, Columbus, Ohio 43202.

Discussion Group

An informal discussion group for stepparents and spouses, led by professional counselors; meets twice monthly; no charge.

Classes, Seminars, and Workshops

Classes for stepparents, spouses, and children, covering such topics as: "The Myth of Instant Love," "The Discipline Dilemma," and "Blended Parenting."

Counseling and Consultation

Family, couple, and individual counseling for defining and clarifying your stepfamily's dynamics, handling adjustment issues, establishing your family goals, strengthening stepparenting skills.

Speakers Bureau

Talks, lectures, seminars, and workshops for community, church, educational, and professional groups covering all aspects of stepfamily life. Radio and TV news and talk-show appearances.

For information about STEP UP resources, or to book the authors for speaking engagements, call 614-268-1094.

ADDITIONAL INFORMATION

If you would like more information about this topic or support for your stepfamily . . .

Contact:

The Stepfamily Foundation
333 West End Avenue
New York, NY 10023

The Stepfamily Association
Suite 212
215 Centennial Mall South
Lincoln, NE   68508

Read:

1. Step Parenting, by J. Lofas with D. Sova.
2. Stepkids: A Survival Guide For Teenagers In Stepfamilies, by A. Getsoff and C. McClenahan.
3. Step-Mothering: Another Kind of Love, by P. Ketover Prilik.
4. How To Live With Other People's Children, by J. and W. Noble.

5. <u>How To Win As A Stepfamily</u>, by E. and J. Visher.
6. <u>Stepfather: Men and Women Talk About Problems In Joining A Family</u>, by T. Gorman.
7. <u>The Stepfamily: Living, Loving, and Learning</u>, by E. Einstein.
8. <u>Second Marriage: Make It Happy! Make It Last</u>, by R. B. Stuart and B. Jacobson.
9. <u>Treating The Remarried Family</u>, by C. Sager (et al).
10. <u>The Boys and Girls Book About Stepfamilies</u>, by R. Gardner
11. <u>Strengthening Your Stepfamily</u>, by E. Einstein and L. Albert.

ABOUT THE AUTHORS

STEVE WILSON, M.A., Licensed Psychologist, psychotherapist and Clinical Director of Ohio Professional Counseling Services, Inc., Columbus, Ohio. Practicing psychology since 1964, Steve became a stepson at the age of 25, four years after his mother's death. He became a stepfather in 1983 when he married Pam. An expert in the area of humor and psychology, Steve is known throughout North America as "The Joyologist," and is the author of two books on that subject: "Eat Dessert First" and "The Art of Mixing Work And Play" (Advocate Publishing Group, Pickerington, Ohio). He is a member of the Ohio Psychological Association, The American Association for Therapeutic Humor, and The National Speakers Association.

ALAN DUPRE-CLARK, D.Min., L.P.C.C., is no stranger to stepfamilies, having experienced his own stepfamily first-hand as a stepfather for more than 10 years. Alan is a Licensed Professional Clinical Counselor, marriage and family therapist, and educator with more than 15 years of professional experience. Since 1988 he has been a coordinator of the STEP-UP program for Ohio Professional Counseling Services, Inc., Columbus, Ohio, and co-leader of a support group for spouses in stepfamilies. He has served as family therapist and Supervisor of Clinical Staff for the Children's Mental Health Center, Columbus, Ohio, and is a clinical member of the American Association for Marriage and Family Therapy.

M. KAREN KEGELMEYER, M.S., L.P.C., brings a blend of personal and professional expertise with stepfamilies. Karen, like an increasing number of people, became a stepdaughter during her adult years. A Licensed Professional Counselor, in practice since 1977, she conducts workshops and classes for organizations, professional and community groups, and since 1988, has been a coordinator of the STEP-UP program for Ohio Professional Counseling Services, Inc., Columbus, Ohio, and co-leader of a support group for spouses in stepfamilies. She holds memberships in The Ohio Psychological Association and The Ohio Association for Counseling and Development.

THREE WAYS TO ORDER ADDITIONAL COPIES OF

"Remarried With Children"

#1 .... Phone your order to 1-800-669-5233 (VISA/MasterCard only).

#2 ..... Complete the order form on the following page and FAX to 614-263-5233 (VISA/ MasterCard only).

#3 ..... Complete the order form on the following page and mail it with check or money order to:

O.P.C.S., Inc.
Suite 120
3400 N. High Street
Columbus, Ohio 43202

YOUR NAME:_____

ADDRESS:_____

CITY:_____STATE:_____ZIP:_____

Please send me _____ copies of "Remarried With Children" at $8.95 each .... $_____
Shipping and handling ....$_____
Ohio residents add 5.75% sales tax ....$_____
        TOTAL enclosed...$_____

(Add $2.00 Shipping and Handling for the first book and $1.00 for each additional book shipped to the same address.)

Charge to my credit card #_____

MasterCard____ VISA____

Signature_____Expiration Date_____

Please send a gift copy of "Remarried With Children" to:

NAME: _____
ADDRESS: _____
CITY: _____ STATE: _____ ZIP: _____
Payment enclosed $ _____